TREASU...
Fanny Crosby

BARBOUR
PUBLISHING

© 2003 by Barbour Publishing, Inc.

ISBN 1-58660-734-0

Cover image © GettyOne, Inc.

This book was excerpted from the title *Treasures from Fanny Crosby: Blessed Assurance,* published by Barbour Books.

Published by Barbour Publishing, Inc., P.O. Box 719, Uhrichsville, Ohio 44683, www.barbourbooks.com

Member of the
Evangelical Christian
Publishers Association

Printed in the United States of America.
5 4 3 2 1

Contents

Introduction

I am Thine, O Lord, I have heard Thy voice,
And it told Thy love to me;
But I long to rise in the arms of faith
And be closer drawn to Thee.

*S*he was physically blinded at a young age,
but Fanny Crosby developed a spiritual vision
like few others. Over the past century, untold
numbers have sung her heartfelt hymns of praise to
God, and her words still bless believers today.

Fanny Crosby never complained about the hard-
ships of life; she simply looked to Jesus. Her attitude
is best summed up by a conversation she had with
a minister. "Do you know," she said, "that if at birth
I had been able to make one petition, it would
have been that I should be born blind?" "Why?"
asked the pastor in surprise. "Because when I get to
heaven," she responded, "the first face that shall
ever gladden my sight will be that of my Savior!"

This book, *Treasures from Fanny Crosby*, contains
topically organized selections from her extensive
hymn writing, as well as comments by and about

this queen of sacred song. You'll find encouragement and challenge in the words of Fanny Crosby, and a deeper insight into the Lord she knew and loved so well.

Comfort in God

And stood at his feet behind him weeping,
and began to wash his feet with tears,
and did wipe them with the hairs of her head,
and kissed his feet,
and anointed them with the ointment.

LUKE 7:38

Sinner, how thy heart is troubled,
God is coming very near;
Do not hide thy deep emotion,
Do not check that falling tear.

And I said, Oh that I had wings like a dove!
for then would I fly away, and be at rest.

PSALM 55:6

Hide me, when the storm is raging
O'er life's troubled sea;
Like a dove on ocean's billows,
O let me fly to Thee.

Also now, behold, my witness is in heaven,
and my record is on high.
My friends scorn me: but mine eye
poureth out tears unto God.

JOB 16:19–20

Hide me, when my heart is breaking
With its weight of woe;
When in tears I seek comfort
Thou canst alone bestow.

❦

O satisfy us early with thy mercy;
that we may rejoice and
be glad all our days.

PSALM 90:14

O child of God, He loveth thee,
and thou art all His own;
With gentle hand He leadeth thee,
thou dost not walk alone;
And though thou watchest wearily
the long and stormy night,
Yet in the morning joy will come,
and fill thy soul with light.

The people which sat in darkness
    saw great light;
and to them which sat in the region
and shadow of death light is sprung up.

MATTHEW 4:16

Redeemed, and so happy in Jesus,
No language my rapture can tell;
I know that the light of His presence
With me doth continually dwell.

I will also praise thee with the psaltery,
    even thy truth, O my God: unto thee
        will I sing with the harp,
        O thou Holy One of Israel.

PSALM 71:22

Down in the human heart,
    crushed by the tempter,
Feelings lie buried that grace can restore;
    Touched by a loving heart,
    wakened by kindness,
Chords that were broken
    will vibrate once more.

And they shall come from the east,
and from the west, and from the north,
and from the south, and shall sit down
in the kingdom of God.

LUKE 13:29

Room at the blessed feast God has prepared,
Room where the bread of life millions
    have shared;
Room where the smiles of love tenderly fall;
Room in Thy arms, O Christ, room,
room for all.

Come unto me,
all ye that labour and are heavy laden,
and I will give you rest.

MATTHEW 11:28

Perfect submission, all is at rest,
I in my Savior am happy and blessed.
Watching and waiting, looking above,
Filled with His goodness, lost in His love.

The Cross of Jesus

A fugitive and a vagabond
shalt thou be in the earth.

GENESIS 4:12

Wanderer, come, there's room for thee,
At the cross of Jesus;
Come and taste salvation free
At the cross of Jesus.

⬱

And he bearing his cross went forth into
a place called the place of a skull,
which is called in the Hebrew Golgotha:
Where they crucified him, and two other with him,
on either side one, and Jesus in the midst.

JOHN 19:17–18

Blessed cross! precious cross!
There my hopes are twining;
There I see a Father's love
Through a Savior shining.

And he said unto Jesus,
Lord, remember me when thou
comest into thy kingdom.

LUKE 23:42

Come and bring thy burden now
To the cross of Jesus;
Lay thy burning, throbbing brow
At the cross of Jesus.

For the preaching of the cross is to them
that perish foolishness;
but unto us which are saved
it is the power of God.

1 CORINTHIANS 1:18

O what comfort thou wilt find
At the cross of Jesus;
Love thy broken heart will bind
At the cross of Jesus.

But one of the soldiers with a spear
pierced his side, and forthwith came
there out blood and water.

JOHN 19:34

See the crimson waters flow
At the cross of Jesus;
Come and tell thy every woe
At the cross of Jesus.

O taste and see that the LORD is good.

PSALM 34:8

Art thou weary?
Wouldst thou lay thy weight aside?
Then rest thee here, the cross is near;
See where Jesus thy Redeemer bled and died,
Come and taste His mercy here.

Who his own self bare our sins in his
own body on the tree.

1 PETER 2:24

He leadeth me, O joy divine!
The glory His, the cross be mine,
Since He who suffered on the tree
In tender mercy leadeth me.

And many women were there
beholding afar off, which followed
Jesus from Galilee,
ministering unto him.

MATTHEW 27:55

Draw me nearer, nearer blessed Lord,
To the cross where Thou hast died.
Draw me nearer, nearer, nearer blessed Lord,
To Thy precious, bleeding side.

In that day there shall be a fountain
opened to the house of David and
to the inhabitants of Jerusalem for sin
and for uncleanness.

ZECHARIAH 13:1

Jesus, keep me near the cross,
There a precious fountain
Free to all—a healing stream
Flows from Calvary's mountain.

But God forbid that I should glory,
save in the cross of our Lord Jesus Christ.

GALATIANS 6:14

In the cross, in the cross,
Be my glory ever;
Till my raptured soul shall find
Rest beyond the river.

I am the root and
the offspring of David,
and the bright and
morning star.

REVELATION 22:16

Near the cross, a trembling soul,
Love and mercy found me;
There the bright and morning star
Sheds its beams around me.

As the shadow of a great rock
in a weary land.

ISAIAH 32:2

Near the cross! O Lamb of God,
Bring its scenes before me;
Help me walk from day to day,
With its shadows over me.

But he was wounded for our transgressions,
he was bruised for our iniquities:
the chastisement of our peace
was upon him; and with his stripes we are healed.

ISAIAH 53:5

Nearer the cross where Jesus died,
Nearer the fountain's crimson tide,
Nearer my Savior's wounded side,
I am coming nearer, I am coming nearer.

Having made peace through the blood of his cross,
by him to reconcile all things unto himself.

COLOSSIANS 1:20

Heavy laden, sore oppressed,
Love can soothe thy troubled breast;
In the Savior find thy rest;
At the cross there's room!

Eternal Salvation

Who shall separate us from
the love of Christ?

ROMANS 8:35

Blest, blest forever,
No more to sever,
Clasped in eternal love,
Blest, blest forever.

And God shall wipe away all tears from their eyes;
and there shall be no more death,
neither sorrow, nor crying,
neither shall there be any more pain:
for the former things are passed away.

REVELATION 21:4

Only a little while, shadow and sadness,
Then in eternity sunshine and gladness;
Only a little while, then o'er the river,
Home, rest and victor palm, life, joy forever.

For whosoever shall call upon
the name of the Lord shall be saved.

ROMANS 10:13

That precious Name their guiding star,
    its beams will o'er them cast,
And through its power their trusting souls
    shall overcome at last.
The glory cloud will bring them safe
    to yonder palace bright,
Where they shall see Him eye to eye
    and walk with Him in white.

❦

But let all those that put their trust in thee rejoice.

PSALM 5:11

How sweet the hour of praise and prayer,
    When our devotions blend,
And on the wings of faith divine
    Our songs of joy ascend!
'Tis then we hear in tones more clear
    The gracious promise giv'n,
That, though we part from friends on earth,
    We all shall meet in heav'n.

Thou in thy mercy hast led forth the people
which thou hast redeemed: thou hast guided
them in thy strength unto thy holy habitation.

EXODUS 15:13

Redeemed, how I love to proclaim it!
Redeemed by the blood of the Lamb;
Redeemed through His infinite mercy,
His child and forever I am.

In the midst of the street of it,
and on either side of the river,
was there the tree of life,
which bare twelve manner of fruits,
and yielded her fruit every month:
and the leaves of the tree were
for the healing of the nations.

REVELATION 22:2

Meet me there, meet me there,
Where the tree of life is blooming, meet me there;
When the storms of life are o'er,
on the happy golden shore,
Where the faithful part no more, meet me there.

And the street of the city was pure gold,
as it were transparent glass.

REVELATION 21:21

On the happy, golden shore,
    where the faithful part no more,
When the storms of life are o'er, meet me there;
Where the night dissolves away into pure
    and perfect day,
I am going home to stay—meet me there.

He opened the rock,
and the waters gushed out;
they ran in the dry places like a river.

PSALM 105:41

Is my hope on the Rifted Rock,
    Cleft by the Lord for me?
Is my name in the book of life?
    O that my faith could see!

With other my fellowlabourers, whose
names are in the book of life.

PHILIPPIANS 4:3

Can I say, with a trusting heart,
Jesus, Thy will, not mine?
Is my name in the book of life,
Sealed by His blood divine?

And there shall in no wise enter
into it any thing that defileth,
neither whatsoever worketh abomination,
or maketh a lie: but they which are written
in the Lamb's book of life.

REVELATION 21:27

When in death I shall calmly sleep,
Jesus, to wake with Thee,
There my name in the book of life
Grant that my eye may see.

Following Christ

Lead me, O LORD, in thy righteousness.

PSALM 5:8

All the way my Savior leads me—
    O the fullness of His love!
Perfect rest to me is promised
    in my Father's house above.
When my spirit, clothed immortal,
    wings its flight to realms of day,
This my song through endless ages:
    Jesus led me all the way;
This my song through endless ages:
    Jesus led me all the way.

❧❧❧

By faith he sojourned in the land of promise.

HEBREWS 11:9

Thou my everlasting portion,
    more than friend or life to me,
All along my pilgrim journey, Savior,
    let me walk with Thee.

I will call upon the LORD, who is worthy to be praised:
so shall I be saved from mine enemies.

PSALM 18:3

We are traveling on through a world of sin,
Walking in the good old way;
Though our foes are strong
    we have peace within,
Walking in the good old way.

Blessed is every one that feareth the LORD;
that walketh in his ways.

PSALM 128:1–2

We are traveling on in the Master's Name,
    Walking in the good old way;
And we sing His praise with a loud acclaim,
    Walking in the good old way.

But and if ye suffer for
righteousness' sake,
happy are ye.

1 PETER 3:14

Not for ease or worldly pleasure,
    nor for fame my prayer shall be;
Gladly will I toil and suffer,
    only let me walk with Thee.
Close to Thee, close to Thee,
    close to Thee, close to Thee,
Gladly will I toil and suffer,
    only let me walk with Thee.

ᐧᕍᕐᕃ

Let not your heart be troubled:
ye believe in God, believe also in me.

JOHN 14:1

Through each perplexing care and strife,
    That marks the checkered path of life,
        My Savior's guiding hand I see,
        And know that still He leadeth me.

And it came to pass, that,
while they communed together and reasoned,
Jesus himself drew near, and went with them.

LUKE 24:15

With Him, my soul's eternal Guide,
What can I wish or want beside?
In life or death my song shall be,
My loving Savior leadeth me.

And, behold, I am with thee,
and will keep thee in all places whither thou goest, and
will bring thee again into this land;
for I will not leave thee,
until I have done that which I have spoken to thee of.

GENESIS 28:15

Withersoever Thou goest,
Let me Thy footsteps attend;
Jesus, my wonderful Savior,
Loving Redeemer and Friend.

For the LORD thy God is with thee
whithersoever thou goest.

JOSHUA 1:9

There would I be, there would I be,
Thou Who hast labored and sorrowed for me;
Whithersoever Thou goest,
There will I follow Thee.

⧽⧼

And walking in the fear of the Lord,
and in the comfort of the Holy Ghost. . .

ACTS 9:31

We are traveling on with our staff in hand,
Walking in the good old way;
We are pilgrims bound for the heavenly land,
Walking in the good old way.

And the LORD went before them by day
in a pillar of a cloud, to lead them the way;
and by night in a pillar of fire, to give them light;
to go by day and night.

EXODUS 13:21

We are traveling on to the rolling tide,
Walking in the good old way;
But we trust in Him who is still our Guide,
Walking in the good old way.

◈

Dearly beloved, I beseech you as strangers
and pilgrims, abstain from fleshly lusts,
which war against the soul.

1 PETER 2:11

Thou my everlasting portion,
More than friend or life to me,
All along my pilgrim journey,
Savior, let me walk with Thee.

Close to Thee, close to Thee,
All along my pilgrim journey,
Savior, let me walk with Thee.

A man that hath friends must show himself friendly: and there is a friend that sticketh closer than a brother.

Proverbs 18:24

Not for ease or worldly pleasure,
Not for fame my prayer shall be;
Gladly will I toil and suffer,
Only let me walk with Thee.

Yea, though I walk through the valley of the shadow of death, I will fear no evil: for thou art with me.

Psalm 23:4

Lead me through the vale of shadows,
Bear me o'er life's fitful sea;
Then the gate of life eternal
May I enter, Lord, with Thee.

Close to Thee, close to Thee,
Close to Thee, close to Thee;
Then the gate of life eternal
May I enter, Lord, with Thee.

Forgiveness of Sin

And Jesus put forth his hand, and touched him,
saying, I will; be thou clean.
And immediately his leprosy was cleansed.

MATTHEW 8:3

Gracious Lord, Thou canst make me clean;
    Lord, I am pleading still;
Now I hear from Thy lips divine,
    "Child, thou hast faith—I will";
Joy to my soul, great joy has come,
    mourning and tears are o'er;
Sweet are the words of Thy love to me,
    "Go thou, and sin no more."

❧

Whom God hath set forth to be a
propitiation through faith in his blood.

ROMANS 3:25

Hark, He bids thee to the crimson fountain go,
    It flows so free, so pure for thee;
He will wash thee and will make thee white as snow,
    Thou His happy child shalt be.

And they shall walk with me in white.

Revelation 3:4

There is a blood-washed multitude,
 a mighty army strong;
The Lord of hosts their righteousness,
 redeeming love their song.
They follow Christ Whose Name they bear,
 to yonder portals bright,
Where He has said His faithful ones shall walk
 with Him in white.

Lord, if thou wilt,
thou canst make me clean.

Matthew 8:2

Gracious Lord, Thou canst make me clean;
 hide not Thy face from me;
 Sick and faint, as the leper came,
 Jesus, I come to Thee.
Thou canst remove the plague of sin,
 washing my inmost soul;
 Jesus, I come with breaking heart,
 help me and make me whole.

Forasmuch as ye know that ye were
not redeemed with corruptible things. . .
But with the precious blood of Christ.

1 PETER 1:18–19

We all shall meet in heav'n at last,
We all shall meet in heav'n;
Through faith in Jesus' precious blood,
We all shall meet in heav'n.

But Jesus turned him about, and when he saw her,
he said, Daughter, be of good comfort;
thy faith hath made thee whole.
And the woman was made whole from that hour.

MATTHEW 9:22

Lord, I am sinful, Thou undefiled,
Yet dost Thou love and even call me Thy child;
Great is Thy mercy, wondrous to me;
Lord, 'tis my faith that saves me, glory to Thee!

Wash me throughly from mine iniquity,
and cleanse me from my sin.

PSALM 51:2

Every day, every hour,
Let me feel Thy cleansing power;
May Thy tender love to me
Bind me closer, closer, Lord to Thee.

Come now, and let us reason together,
saith the LORD: though your sins be as scarlet,
they shall be as white as snow;
though they be red like crimson,
they shall be as wool.

ISAIAH 1:18

"Though your sins be as scarlet,
they shall be as white as snow;
Though your sins be as scarlet,
they shall be as white as snow;
Though they be red like crimson,
they shall be as wool!"
Though your sins be as scarlet,
though your sins be as scarlet,
They shall be as white as snow,
they shall be as white as snow.

For I will forgive their iniquity, and I will
remember their sin no more.

JEREMIAH 31:34

He'll forgive your transgressions,
    and remember them no more;
He'll forgive your transgressions,
    and remember them no more;
"Look unto Me, ye people,"
    saith the Lord your God!
He'll forgive your transgressions,
    He'll forgive your transgressions,
And remember them no more,
    and remember them no more.

❧

For he will abundantly pardon.

ISAIAH 55:7

O perfect redemption, the purchase of blood,
    To every believer the promise of God;
    The vilest offender who truly believes,
That moment from Jesus a pardon receives.

Holy Living

Redeeming the time,
because the days are evil.

EPHESIANS 5:16

Away! away! for the moments are flying,
Time for us will soon be o'er;
This holy day we will try to improve it,
Ere its light is o'er.

                    I can do all things through Christ
                    which strengtheneth me.

                              PHILIPPIANS 4:13

          A wonderful Savior is Jesus my Lord,
                    He taketh my burden away;
          He holdeth me up, and I shall not be moved,
                    He giveth me strength as my day.

Hope of Glory

The blind receive their sight,
and the lame walk,
the lepers are cleansed.

MATTHEW 11:5

Gracious Lord, Thou canst make me clean;
Speak, and my soul shall live;
O my faith will not let Thee go
Till Thou my sin forgive.

❧

Who is he that condemneth?
It is Christ that died, yea rather,
that is risen again, who is even at
the right hand of God,
who also maketh intercession for us.

ROMANS 8:34

Still at Thy mercy seat, Savior, I fall;
Trusting Thy promise sweet, heard is my call;
Faith wings my soul to Thee; this all my song shall be,
Jesus has died for me, Jesus my all.

Lazarus sleepeth; but I go,
that I may awake him out of sleep.

JOHN 11:11

Yet a little while we linger,
    ere we reach our journey's end;
Yet a little while of labor,
    ere the evening shades descend;
Then we'll lay us down to slumber,
    but the night will soon be o'er;
In the bright, the bright forever,
    we shall wake, to weep no more.

When Christ, who is our life, shall appear,
then shall ye also appear with him in glory.

COLOSSIANS 3:4

I have climbed the rugged mountain,
    On its summit now I stand;
    Hallelujah! hallelujah!
    I have entered Beulah land.

And, behold, there arose a great tempest in the sea,
insomuch that the ship was covered with the waves:
but he was asleep.
And his disciples came to him, and awoke him,
saying, Lord, save us: we perish.

MATTHEW 8:24–25

Gliding o'er life's fitful waters,
Heavy surges sometimes roll;
And we sigh for yonder haven,
For the homeland of the soul.

Verily, verily, I say unto you,
The hour is coming, and now is,
when the dead shall hear
the voice of the Son of God:
and they that hear shall live.

JOHN 5:25

Blessed homeland, ever fair!
Sin can never enter there;
But the soul, to life awaking,
Everlasting bloom shall wear.

For now we see through a glass, darkly;
but then face to face.

1 CORINTHIANS 13:12

Oft we catch a faint reflection,
Of its bright and vernal hills;
And, though distant, how we hail it!
How each heart with rapture thrills!

❦

And I saw a new heaven and a new earth:
for the first heaven and the first earth
were passed away;
and there was no more sea.

REVELATION 21:1

'Tis the weary pilgrim's homeland,
Where each throbbing care shall cease,
And our longings and our yearnings,
Like a wave, be hushed to peace.

And had a wall great and high,
and had twelve gates.

REVELATION 21:12

Lead me through the vale of shadows,
    bear me over life's fitful sea;
Then the gate of life eternal may I enter,
    Lord, with Thee.
Close to Thee, close to Thee,
    close to Thee, close to Thee,
Then the gate of life eternal may I enter,
    Lord, with Thee.

But the throne of God
and of the Lamb shall be in it;
and his servants shall serve him:
And they shall see his face.

REVELATION 22:3–4

By and by, by and by,
We shall all clasp hands in glory by and by.
We shall see our Savior's face,
And adore His wondrous grace,
We shall feel His fond embrace by and by.

Invitation to Salvation

And they shall come from the east, and from the west,
and from the north, and from the south,
and shall sit down in the kingdom of God.

LUKE 13:29

Come, poor sinner, to the blessed, blessed feast,
O hear the call—thy Savior's call;
Haste to meet Him,
　　He will welcome thee His guest,
O rejoice, there's room for all.

❧

And the Spirit and the bride say, Come.
And let him that heareth say, Come.
And let him that is athirst come.
And whosoever will, let him take the water of life freely.

REVELATION 22:17

Whosoever will in that feast may share,
In our Father's house there is bread to spare;
Come to Jesus, He is waiting, waiting now,
Come, O come, there's room for all.

For even Christ our passover is sacrificed for us:
Therefore let us keep the feast.

1 CORINTHIANS 5:7–8

Come to Jesus, and thy burden He will bear,
The feast is spread, lift up thy head;
Come, and rest thee in the Savior's gentle care,
By His love thou shalt be fed.

For whosoever shall call upon the name
of the Lord shall be saved.

ROMANS 10:13

O be saved, His grace is free;
O be saved, He died for thee;
O be saved, He died for thee.

We pray you in Christ's stead,
be ye reconciled to God.

2 CORINTHIANS 5:20

Jesus now is bending o'er thee,
Jesus lowly, meek and mild;
To the Friend Who died to save thee,
Canst thou not be reconciled?

Behold, now is the accepted time; behold,
now is the day of salvation.

2 CORINTHIANS 6:2

Art thou waiting till the morrow?
Thou may'st never see its light;
Come at once—accept His mercy,
He is waiting—come tonight.

I say unto you, that likewise joy shall be in
heaven over one sinner that repenteth,
more than over ninety and nine just persons,
which need no repentance.

LUKE 15:7

Let the angels bear the tidings,
Upward to the courts of heaven;
Let them sing, with holy rapture,
O'er another soul forgiven.

That if thou shalt confess with thy mouth
the Lord Jesus, and shalt believe in thine heart
that God hath raised him from the dead,
thou shalt be saved.

ROMANS 10:9

Only a step to Jesus!
Then why not take it now?
Come, and thy sin confessing,
To Him, thy Savior, bow.

If we confess our sins,
he is faithful and just to forgive us our sins,
and to cleanse us from all unrighteousness.

1 JOHN 1:9

Only a step, only a step,
Come, He waits for thee;
Come, and thy sin confessing,
Thou shalt receive a blessing;
Do not reject the mercy
He freely offers thee.

◈

And when he saw their faith,
he said unto him, Man,
thy sins are forgiven thee.

LUKE 5:20

Only a step to Jesus!
Believe, and thou shalt live;
Lovingly now He's waiting,
And ready to forgive.

But where sin abounded,
grace did much more abound.

ROMANS 5:20

Only a step to Jesus!
A step from sin to grace;
What has thy heart decided?
The moments fly apace.

There came unto him a woman
having an alabaster box of
very precious ointment,
and poured it on his head,
as he sat at meat.

MATTHEW 26:7

Only a step to Jesus!
O why not come and say,
"Gladly to Thee my Savior,
I give myself away."

Praise the Lord

The heavens declare the glory of God;
and the firmament sheweth his handywork.

PSALM 19:1

Praise the Lord, praise the Lord,
Let the earth hear His voice!
Praise the Lord, praise the Lord,
Let the people rejoice!
O come to the Father, through Jesus the Son,
And give Him the glory, great things
He hath done.

How much more shall the blood of Christ,
who through the eternal Spirit
offered himself without spot to God,
purge your conscience from dead works
to serve the living God?

HEBREWS 9:14

Come, Holy Ghost, the blood apply
As Thou hast ne'er before,
That I may shout my Savior's praise
Henceforth and evermore.

So teach us to number our days.

PSALM 90:12

Who has led me all my days?
    Only Thou, my Savior;
Who deserves my highest praise?
    Only Thou, my Savior;
In my weakness Who is strong,
    Who has loved and loved me long,
Who should claim my noblest song?
    Only Thou, my Savior.

❧

Therefore, my beloved brethren,
be ye stedfast, unmoveable,
always abounding in the work of the Lord,
forasmuch as ye know that your labour
is not in vain in the Lord.

1 CORINTHIANS 15:58

To our Father, and our Savior,
To the Spirit, Three in One,
We shall sing glad songs of triumph
When our harvest work is done.

I beheld till the thrones were cast down,
and the Ancient of days did sit,
whose garment was white as snow,
and the hair of his head like the pure wool.

DANIEL 7:9

Blessed Redeemer, wonderful Savior,
Fountain of wisdom, Ancient of Days,
Hope of the faithful, Light of all ages,
Jesus my Savior, Thee will I praise.

Then shall the righteous shine forth as the sun
in the kingdom of their Father.

MATTHEW 13:43

Conquering now and still to conquer,
who is this wonderful King?
Whence are the armies which He leadeth,
while of His glory they sing?
He is our Lord and Redeemer,
Savior and Monarch divine;
They are the stars that forever bright
in His kingdom shall shine.

And he leaping up stood, and walked,
and entered with them into the temple,
walking, and leaping, and praising God.

ACTS 3:8

He leadeth me, he leadeth me,
Let this my theme of rapture be!
He leadeth me, He leadeth me,
My Savior's guiding hand I see.

He brought streams also out of the rock,
and caused waters to run down like rivers.

PSALM 78:16

A wonderful Savior is Jesus my Lord,
A wonderful Savior to me;
He hideth my soul in the cleft of the rock,
Where rivers of pleasure I see.

Preaching the Gospel

And ye shall hallow the fiftieth year,
and proclaim liberty throughout
all the land unto all the inhabitants thereof:
it shall be a jubile unto you.

LEVITICUS 25:10

Awake! Awake! the Master now is calling us,
Arise! Arise! And, trusting in His Word,
Go forth! Go forth! Proclaim the year of jubilee,
And take the cross, the blessed cross of Christ
     our Lord.

And when they had lifted up their eyes,
     they saw no man, save Jesus only.

MATTHEW 17:8

Glory, glory, hear the everlasting throng,
Shout, "Hosanna!" while we boldly march along;
     Faithful soldiers here below,
          only Jesus will we know;
Shouting, "Free salvation!" over the world we go.

And a vision appeared to Paul in the night;
there stood a man of Macedonia,
and prayed him, saying,
Come over into Macedonia, and help us.

ACTS 16:9

A cry for light from dying ones in heathen lands;
It comes, it comes across the ocean's foam;
Then haste! Oh, haste to spread the words
of truth abroad,
Forgetting not the starving poor at home,
dear home.

For the kingdom of heaven is like
unto a man that is an householder,
which went out early in the morning
to hire labourers into his vineyard.

MATTHEW 20:1

Away! away! not a moment to lose,
Haste we now with footstep free,
Where those who love in the vineyard to labor,
Wait for you and me.

He keepeth back his soul from the pit,
and his life from perishing by the sword.

JOB 33:18

Rescue the perishing, care for the dying,
Snatch them in pity from sin and the grave;
Weep over the erring one, lift up the fallen,
Tell them of Jesus, the mighty to save.

⚬⚬⚬

But Peter, standing up with the eleven,
lifted up his voice, and said unto them,
Ye men of Judaea. . .hearken to my words.

ACTS 2:14

Though they are slighting Him,
still He is waiting,
Waiting the penitent child to receive;
Plead with them earnestly,
plead with them gently;
He will forgive if they only believe.

He that winneth souls is wise.

PROVERBS 11:30

Rescue the perishing, duty demands it;
Strength for thy labor the Lord will provide;
Back to the narrow way patiently win them;
Tell the poor wanderer a Savior has died.

Go ye therefore, and teach all nations.

MATTHEW 28:19

Speed away, speed away, on your mission of light,
To the lands that are lying in darkness and night;
'Tis the Master's command;
go ye forth in His name,
The wonderful Gospel of Jesus proclaim.

And sent his servant at supper time
to say to them that were bidden, Come;
for all things are now ready.

LUKE 14:17

To the souls by the tempter in bondage oppressed;
For the Savior has purchased their ransom
    from sin,
And the banquet is ready, O gather them in.

Come unto me,
all ye that labour and are heavy laden,
and I will give you rest.

MATTHEW 11:28

To the nations that know
not the voice of the Lord;
Take the wings of the morning
and fly o'er the wave,
In the strength of your Master
the lost ones to save;
He is calling once more, not at moment's delay,
Speed away, speed away, speed away.
Speed away, speed away with the message of rest.

And they talked together of all these things
which had happened.

LUKE 24:14

Tell me the story of Jesus,
 write on my heart every word.
Tell me the story most precious,
 sweetest that ever was heard.
Tell how the angels in chorus,
 sang as they welcomed His birth.
"Glory to God in the highest!
 Peace and good tidings to earth."

Then was Jesus led up of the spirit into the
wilderness to be tempted of the devil.

MATTHEW 4:1

Fasting alone in the desert,
 tell of the days that are past.
How for our sins He was tempted,
 yet was triumphant at last.
Tell of the years of His labor,
 tell of the sorrow He bore.
He was despised and afflicted,
 homeless, rejected and poor.

Refreshed by God

For they drank of that spiritual Rock that
followed them: and that Rock was Christ.

1 CORINTHIANS 10:4

All the way my Savior leads me—
    cheers each winding path I tread,
Gives me grace for every trial,
    feeds me with the living bread.
Though my weary steps may falter
    and my soul athirst may be,
Gushing from the Rock before me, Lo!
    A spring of joy I see.

❦

Grace to you and peace from God our Father,
and the Lord Jesus Christ.

ROMANS 1:7

Never be sad or desponding,
If thou hast faith to believe.
Grace, for the duties before thee,
Ask of thy God and receive.

And I will pray the Father,
and he shall give you another Comforter,
that he may abide with you for ever.

JOHN 14:16

Come, Holy Comforter, Presence Divine,
Now in our longing hearts graciously shine;
O for Thy mighty power! O for a blessed shower,
Filling this hallowed hour with joy divine!

❧

But whosoever drinketh of the water
that I shall give him shall never thirst;
but the water that I shall give him
shall be in him a well of water
springing up into everlasting life.

JOHN 4:14

There, beside the wells of water
From celestial springs,
Celestial springs that flow,
There the everlasting kindness
Of our Savior we shall know.

Repentance

Know ye not, that to whom ye yield yourselves
servants to obey, his servants ye are to whom
ye obey; whether of sin unto death,
or of obedience unto righteousness?

ROMANS 6:16

The way of transgression that leads unto death,
Oh, why will you longer pursue?
How can you reject the sweet message of love
That offers full pardon for you?

⬡

Who shall separate us from the love of Christ? shall
tribulation, or distress, or persecution,
or famine, or nakedness, or peril, or sword?

ROMANS 8:35

Be warned of your danger; escape to the cross;
Your only salvation is there;
Believe, and that moment the Spirit of grace
Will answer your penitent prayer.

I came not to call the righteous,
but sinners to repentance.

LUKE 5:32

I've wandered far away o'er mountains cold,
I've wandered far away from home;
O take me now, and bring me to Thy fold,
Come, Great Deliverer, come.

For in the time of trouble he shall hide me
in his pavilion: in the secret of his
tabernacle shall he hide me; he shall
set me up upon a rock.

PSALM 27:5

I have no place, no shelter from the night,
Come, Great Deliverer, come;
One look from Thee would give me life and light,
Come, Great Deliverer, come.

Turn thee unto me, and have mercy upon me;
for I am desolate and afflicted.

PSALM 25:16

My path is lone, and weary are my feet,
Come, Great Deliverer, come;
Mine eyes look up Thy loving smile to meet,
Come, Great Deliverer, come.

All that the Father giveth me shall
come to me; and him that cometh to me
I will in no wise cast out.

JOHN 6:37

Thou wilt not spurn contrition's broken sigh,
Come, Great Deliverer, come.
Regard my prayer, and hear my humble cry,
Come, Great Deliverer, come.

And he said, Lord, I believe.
And he worshipped him.

JOHN 9:38

Gracious Lord, Thou canst make me clean;
    weary and sad am I;
Bending low at Thy sacred feet,
    hear my repentant cry;
Faith in Thy Word has led me here,
    faith cannot plead in vain;
Lord, I believe; O cleanse me now,
    wash me from every stain.

⌘

If we confess our sins, he is faithful
and just to forgive us our sins,
and to cleanse us from all unrighteousness.

1 JOHN 1:9

Lord, at Thy mercy seat, humbly I fall;
Pleading Thy promise sweet, Lord, hear my call;
Now let Thy work begin, oh,
make me pure within,
Cleanse me from every sin, Jesus, my all.

But God commendeth his love toward us,
in that, while we were yet sinners,
Christ died for us.

ROMANS 5:8

Tears of repentant grief, silently fall;
Help Thou my unbelief, hear Thou my call;
Oh, how I pine for Thee! 'Tis all my hope
    and plea:
Jesus has died for me, Jesus, my all.

From that time Jesus began to preach,
and to say, Repent:
for the kingdom of heaven is at hand.

MATTHEW 4:17

Hear the voice that entreats you,
O return ye unto God!
He is of great compassion, and of wondrous love;
Hear the voice that entreats you,
hear the voice that entreats you,
O return ye unto God! O return ye unto God!

63

Return of Christ

Then we which are alive and remain shall be caught up
together with them in the clouds
to meet the Lord in the air:
and so shall we ever be with the Lord.

1 THESSALONIANS 4:17

When clothed in His brightness,
    transported I rise
To meet Him in clouds of the sky,
His perfect salvation, His wonderful love
I'll shout with the millions on high.

This same Jesus, which is taken up from
you into heaven, shall so come in like manner
as ye have seen him go into heaven.

ACTS 1:11

He is coming, the "Man of Sorrows,"
    Now exalted on high;
He is coming with loud hosannas,
    In the clouds of the sky.

The kingdoms of this world are become
the kingdoms of our Lord, and of his Christ;
and he shall reign for ever and ever.

REVELATION 11:15

He is coming, our loving Savior,
Blessed Lamb that was slain;
In the glory of God the Father,
On the earth He shall reign.

I heard a great voice of much people in heaven,
saying, Alleluia; Salvation, and glory,
and honour, and power,
unto the Lord our God.

REVELATION 19:1

He is coming, our Lord and Master,
Our Redeemer and King;
We shall see Him in all His beauty,
And His praise we shall sing.

Safety in Christ

I am the door: by me if any man enter in,
he shall be saved, and shall go in and out,
and find pasture.

JOHN 10:9

O Church of God, extend thy kind, maternal arms,
To save the lost on mountains dark and cold;
Reach out thy hand with loving smile to
    rescue them,
And bring them to the shelter of the Savior's fold.

❧

For thou hast been a strength to the poor,
a strength to the needy in his distress,
a refuge from the storm.

ISAIAH 25:4

Blessed Redeemer, Thou art my refuge,
Under Thy watch-care, safe I shall be;
Gladly adoring, joyfully trusting,
Still I am coming closer to Thee.

And a man shall be as an hiding place from
the wind, and a covert from the tempest.

ISAIAH 32:2

Blessed Redeemer, gracious and tender,
Now and forever dwell Thou in me;
Thou, my Protector, Shield and Defender,
Draw me and keep me closer to Thee.

And I give unto them eternal life;
and they shall never perish,
neither shall any man pluck
them out of my hand.

JOHN 10:28

We shall all clasp hands in glory by and by;
We shall tell redemption's story by and by;
When the voyage of life is past
We shall reach the port at last,
And our anchor safely cast by and by.

As rivers of water in a dry place,
as the shadow of a great rock
in a weary land.

ISAIAH 32:2

He hideth my soul in the cleft of the rock
That shadows a dry, thirsty land;
He hideth my life with the depths of His love,
And covers me there with His hand,
And covers me there with His hand.

For in the time of trouble he shall hide me
in his pavilion: in the secret of
his tabernacle shall he hide me; he shall
set me up upon a rock.

PSALM 27:5

Hide me, hide me,
O blessed Savior, hide me;
O Savior, keep me,
Safely, O Lord, with Thee.

Then Peter, turning about, seeth the disciple
whom Jesus loved following; which also
leaned on his breast at supper.

JOHN 21:20

Safe in the arms of Jesus, safe on His gentle breast,
There by His love o'ershaded, sweetly my soul
    shall rest.
Hark! 'tis the voice of angels, borne in a song
    to me.
Over the fields of glory, over the jasper sea.

Be careful for nothing.

PHILIPPIANS 4:6

Safe in the arms of Jesus,
    safe from corroding care,
Safe from the world's temptations,
    sin cannot harm me there.
Free from the blight of sorrow,
    free from my doubts and fears;
Only a few more trials, only a few more tears!

But let all those that put their trust
in thee rejoice: let them ever shout for joy,
because thou defendest them.

PSALM 5:11

Jesus, my heart's dear refuge, Jesus has died for me;
Firm on the Rock of Ages, ever my trust shall be.
Here let me wait with patience,
    wait till the night is over;
Wait till I see the morning break on
    the golden shore.

For this my son was dead, and is alive again;
he was lost, and is found.

LUKE 15:24

Lost, but found, my sins forgiven,
Child of God and heir of Heaven;
Lost, but found, what joy is mine!
Thou dost cleanse and keep me Thine.

Seeking the Lord

Come unto me,
all ye that labour and are heavy laden,
and I will give you rest.

MATTHEW 11:28

Blessed Redeemer, full of compassion,
Great is Thy mercy, boundless and free;
Now in my weakness, seeking Thy favor,
Lord, I am coming closer to Thee.

❦

They shall praise the LORD that seek him.

PSALM 22:26

Here from the world we turn, Jesus to seek;
Here may His loving voice tenderly speak!
Jesus, our dearest Friend,
while at Thy feet we bend,
O let Thy smile descend! 'Tis Thee we seek.

Draw me.

SONG OF SONGS 1:4

I am Thine, O Lord, I have heard Thy voice,
And it told Thy love to me;
But I long to rise in the arms of faith
And be closer drawn to Thee.

❦

I laboured more abundantly than they all:
yet not I, but the grace of God
which was with me.

1 CORINTHIANS 15:10

Consecrate me now to Thy service, Lord,
By the power of grace divine;
Let my soul look up with a steadfast hope,
And my will be lost in Thine.

And the LORD spake unto Moses face to face,
as a man speaketh unto his friend.

EXODUS 33:11

O the pure delight of a single hour
That before Thy throne I spend,
When I kneel in prayer, and with Thee, my God
I commune as friend with friend!

⎯⎯⎯✦⎯⎯⎯

Hide me under the shadow of thy wings.

PSALM 17:8

Hide me, O my Savior, hide me
In Thy holy place;
Resting there beneath Thy glory,
O let me see Thy face.

Know ye not your own selves,
how that Jesus Christ is in you?

2 CORINTHIANS 13:5

More like Jesus would I be,
    let my Savior dwell in me;
Fill my soul with peace and love,
    make me gentle as a dove;
More like Jesus, while I go,
    pilgrim in this world below;
Poor in spirit would I be;
    let my Savior dwell in me.

∗∗∗

Christ in you, the hope of glory.

COLOSSIANS 1:27

If He hears the raven's cry,
    if His ever watchful eye
Marks the sparrows when they fall,
    surely He will hear my call:
He will teach me how to live,
    all my sinful thoughts forgive;
Pure in heart I still would be;
    let my Savior dwell in me.

I am crucified with Christ: nevertheless I live;
yet not I, but Christ liveth in me.

GALATIANS 2:20

More like Jesus when I pray,
    more like Jesus day by day;
May I rest me by His side,
    where the tranquil waters glide:
Born of Him, through grace renewed,
    by His love my will subdued,
Rich in faith I still would be;
    let my Savior dwell in me.

To him that overcometh will I give
    to eat of the hidden manna.

REVELATION 2:17

Nearer the Christian's mercy seat,
    I am coming nearer;
Feasting my soul on manna sweet
    I am coming nearer.

Trust in Christ

Thou wilt keep him in perfect peace, whose mind is stayed on thee: because he trusteth in thee.

ISAIAH 26:3

All the way my Savior leads me—
    what have I to ask beside?
Can I doubt His tender mercy,
    Who through life has been my guide?
Heavenly peace, divinest comfort,
    here by faith in Him to dwell!
For I know, whatever befall me,
    Jesus doeth all things well.

Trust in the LORD with all thine heart; and lean not unto thine own understanding.

PROVERBS 3:5

When my way is hedged about me,
    hedged with thorns of care;
When the cross I loved so dearly,
    seems too hard to bear;
When my heart is bowed with sorrow,
    and no light I see—
Lord, Thy tender mercy pleading,
    let me lean on Thee.

They shall run, and not be weary; and
they shall walk, and not faint.

ISAIAH 40:31

O, for faith to cast behind me every sad
    complaint—
Faith to run and not be weary, walk and
    never faint;
Thou dost know and feel my weakness,
    Savior look on me;
Now Thy tender mercy pleading,
    let me lean on Thee.

Yet will they lean upon the LORD,
and say, Is not the LORD among us?
none evil can come upon us.

MICAH 3:11

Closer let Thine arms enfold me,
    closer to Thy breast
Draw my weary, trembling spirit,
    calm its doubts to rest;
Give me strength for every burden
    Thou hast borne for me;
Lord, Thy tender mercy pleading,
    let me lean on Thee.

And at midnight Paul and Silas prayed,
and sang praises unto God:
and the prisoners heard them.

ACTS 16:25

Never give up, never give up,
Never give up to thy sorrows,
Jesus will bid them depart.
Trust in the Lord, trust in the Lord,
Sing when your trials are greatest,
Trust in the Lord and take heart.

With whom my hand shall be established:
mine arm also shall strengthen him.

PSALM 89:21

Never be sad or desponding,
Lean on the arm of thy Lord;
Dwell in the depths of His mercy,
Thou shalt receive thy reward.

Weeping may endure for a night,
but joy cometh in the morning.

PSALM 30:5

O child of God, wait patiently when dark
    thy path may be,
And let thy faith lean trustingly on Him
    Who cares for Thee;
And though the clouds hang drearily upon
    the brow of night,
Yet in the morning joy will come,
    and fill thy soul with light.

Forasmuch as ye know that ye were not
redeemed with corruptible things,
as silver and gold. . .
But with the precious blood of Christ.

1 PETER 1:18–19

Savior, more than life to me,
I am clinging, clinging, close to Thee;
Let Thy precious blood applied,
Keep me ever, ever near Thy side.

Lead me into the
land of uprightness.

PSALM 143:10

Through this changing world below,
Lead me gently, gently as I go;
Trusting Thee, I cannot stray,
I can never, never lose my way.

❧

Though your sins be as scarlet,
they shall be as white as snow;
though they be red like crimson,
they shall be as wool.

ISAIAH 1:18

What I am, Thine eye can see,
Yet I come, O Lord, to Thee.
Though my sins are crimson red,
Yet for me Thy blood was shed.

For Christ also hath once suffered for sins,
the just for the unjust, that he might
bring us to God.

1 PETER 3:18

This my plea, my only plea:
Through Thy offering once for me,
I may cast myself on Thee,
Jesus, my Redeemer.

❧

Set me as a seal upon thine heart.

SONG OF SONGS 8:6

As I am, I seek Thy face,
Kneeling at the door of grace;
O forgive this heart of mine,
Cleanse me now and seal me Thine.

Victory in Christ

And I saw, and behold a white horse:
and he that sat on him had a bow;
and a crown was given unto him:
and he went forth conquering,
and to conquer.

REVELATION 6:2

Conquering now and still to conquer,
    rideth a King in His might;
Leading the host of all the faithful into
    the midst of the fight;
See them with courage advancing,
    clad in their brilliant array,
Shouting the name of their Leader,
    hear them exultingly say:

Not to the strong is the battle,
Not to the swift is the race,
Yet to the true and the faithful
Victory is promised through grace.

Blessed is the man that endureth temptation:
for when he is tried,
he shall receive the crown of life,
which the Lord hath promised
to them that love him.

JAMES 1:12

O the friends that now are waiting,
In the cloudless realms of day,
Who are calling me to follow
Where their steps have led the way;
They have laid aside their armor,
And their earthly course is run;
They have kept the faith with patience
And their crown of life is won.

Worship of God

For the Son of man is Lord
even of the sabbath day.

MATTHEW 12:8

Away! away! where the angels are bending
Lightly o'er the house of prayer.
Glad hymns of praise to the Lord of the Sabbath,
Sweetly echo there.

Is there no balm in Gilead?

JEREMIAH 8:22

'Tis the blessed hour of prayer,
when our hearts lowly bend,
And we gather to Jesus, our Savior and friend;
If we come to Him in faith, His protection to share,
What a balm for the weary,
O how sweet to be there!

Casting all your care upon him;
for he careth for you.

1 PETER 5:7

'Tis the blessed hour of prayer,
    when the Savior draws near,
With a tender compassion His children to hear;
When He tells us we may cast at His feet
    every care,
What a balm for the weary,
    O how sweet to be there!

For we have not an high priest which
cannot be touched with the feeling
of our infirmities.

HEBREWS 4:15

'Tis the blessed hour of prayer,
    when the tempted and tried
To the Savior Who loves them their sorrow confide;
With a sympathizing heart He removes every care;
    What a balm for the weary,
      O how sweet to be there!

Even as the Son of man came
not to be ministered unto,
but to minister, and to give his life
a ransom for many.

MATTHEW 20:28

To God be the glory, great things He has done;
So loved He the world that He gave us His Son,
Who yielded His life an atonement for sin,
And opened the life gate that all may go in.

Now unto the King eternal, immortal,
invisible, the only wise God,
be honour and glory for ever and ever. Amen.

1 TIMOTHY 1:17

King eternal, blessed be His Name!
So may His children gladly adore Him;
When in heav'n we join the happy strain,
When we cast our bright crowns before Him:
There in His likeness joyful awaking,
There we shall see Him, there shall we sing.

Quotes

Long before he became the head of the nation, [Grover Cleveland] was employed in the modest position of secretary to the Institution of the Blind in which Miss Crosby was a teacher. They became close friends, and he copied many of her poems for her. Long afterward, when he had become President, he wrote her a beautiful tribute: "It is more than fifty years ago that our acquaintance and friendship began, and ever since that time I have watched your continuous and disinterested labor in uplifting humanity and pointing out the way to an appreciation of God's goodness and mercy."

❧

My ambition was boundless and my desires were intent to live for some great purpose in the world and to make for myself a name that should endure.

I seem to have been led little by little, toward my work; and I believe that the same fact will appear in the life of anyone who will cultivate such powers as God has given him, and then go on, bravely, quietly, but persistently, doing such work as comes to his hands.

❧

If I were given a little time in which to do it, I could take down from the shelves of my memory hundreds if not thousands of hymns that I have written in the sixty years during which I have been praising my Redeemer through this medium of song.

❧

In successful songs, words and music must harmonize not only in number of syllables but in subject matter, and especially in accent. Thus melodies tell their own tale, and it is the purpose of the poet to interpret the musical story into language. If the melody says nothing to the poet, his words will never agree with the music.

The most enduring hymns are born in the silences of the soul and nothing must be allowed to intrude while they are being framed into language. Some of the sweetest melodies of the heart never see the light of the printed page. Sometimes the song without words has a deeper meaning than the most elaborate combinations of words and music.

That some of my hymns have been dictated by the blessed Holy Spirit, I have no doubt. That others have been the result of deep meditation, I know to be true. But that the poet has any right to claim special merit for himself is certainly presumptuous. I have sometimes felt that there is a deep and clear well of inspiration from which one may draw the sparkling draughts that are so essential to good poetry. At times the burden of inspiration is so heavy that the author himself cannot find words beautiful enough or thoughts deep enough for its expression.

Most of my poems have been written during the long night watches when the distractions of the day could not interfere with the rapid flow of thought. It has been my custom to hold a little book in my hand; and somehow or other the words seem to come more promptly when I am so engaged.

❧

It seemed intended by the blessed providence of God that I should be blind all my life, and I thank Him for the dispensation. If perfect earthly sight were offered me tomorrow, I would not accept it. I might not have sung hymns to the praise of God if I had been distracted by the beautiful and interesting things about me.

❧

When I look down the avenue of these ninety years, I find that I have been interested in everything advanced for the welfare of mankind.

❧

I have made up my mind never to become a disagreeable old woman, and always to take cheer and sunshine with me.

❧

Oh, what a happy soul I am,
Although I cannot see!
I am resolved that in this world
Contented I will be.

How many blessings I enjoy
That other people don't;
To weep and sigh because I'm blind,
I cannot and I won't!

On April 30, 1868, Dr. W. H. Doane came into my house and said, "I have exactly forty minutes before my train leaves for Cincinnati. Here is a melody. Can you write words for it?" I replied that I would see what I could do. Then followed a space of twenty minutes during which I was wholly unconscious of all else except the work I was doing. At the end of that time I recited the words to "Safe in the Arms of Jesus." Mr. Doane copied them, and had time to catch his train.

❧

The hymn ["Saved by Grace"]. . .was called into being through. . .a sermon preached by Dr. Howard Crosby who was a distant relative and dear friend of mine. He said that no Christian should fear death, for if each of us was faithful to the grace given us by Christ, the same grace that teaches us how to live would also teach us how to die. His remarks were afterward published in a newspaper, and they were read to me by Mr. Biglow. Not many hours after I heard them I began to write the hymn.

I am fully aware of the immense debt I owe to those numberless friends. . .especially to that dear Friend of us all, who is our light and life.

Near the humble cottage in which I lived for the first few years of my childhood ran a tiny brook, one of the branches of the Croton River; and the music of its waters was so sweet in my ears that I fancied it was not to be surpassed by any of the grand melodies in the great world beyond our little valley.

There are forms that flit before me,
There are tones I yet recall;
But the voice of gentle grandma
I remember best of all.

In her loving arms she held me,
And beneath her patient care
I was borne away to dreamland
In her dear old rocking chair.

When I had exhausted all the methods of entertainment at my command, mother came to me and said, "I think I have found something that will please you." Then she placed in my arms a tiny lamb that had lost its mother; and the little orphan at once was received into the warmth of my affections. Through the fields and meadows we romped when the days were warm; occasionally I fell asleep under a great oak tree with my pet at my side.

❧

When I remember his mercy and lovingkindness; when I have been blessed above the common lot of mortals; and when happiness has touched the deep places of my soul—how can I repine? And I have often thought of the passage of Scripture: "The light of the body is the eye: if therefore thine eye, be single thy whole body shall be full of light."

Among the great number of hymns that I have written—eight thousand perhaps—it is not always possible for me to remember even the best of them. . . . I did not recognize ["Hide Me, O My Savior, Hide Me"] as my own production. . .

"Mr. Sankey," I said, "now you must tell me who is the author of 'Hide Me, O My Savior.' "

"Really," he replied, "don't you recall who wrote that hymn? You ought to remember, for you are the guilty one."

Inspirational Library

Beautiful purse/pocket-size editions of Christian classics bound in flexible leatherette. These books make thoughtful gifts for everyone on your list, including yourself!

When I'm on My Knees   The highly popular collection of devotional thoughts on prayer, especially for women.
　　Flexible Leatherette $4.99

The Bible Promise Book   Over 1,000 promises from God's Word arranged by topic. What does God promise about matters like: Anger, Illness, Jealousy, Love, Money, Old Age, and Mercy? Find out in this book!
　　Flexible Leatherette $3.99

Daily Wisdom for Women   A daily devotional for women seeking biblical wisdom to apply to their lives. Scripture taken from the New American Standard Version of the Bible.
　　Flexible Leatherette $4.99

My Daily Prayer Journal   Each page is dated and features a Scripture verse and ample room for you to record your thoughts, prayers, and praises. One page for each day of the year.
　　Flexible Leatherette $4.99

Available wherever books are sold.
Or order from:

Barbour Publishing, Inc.
P.O. Box 719
Uhrichsville, OH 44683
www.barbourbooks.com

If you order by mail, add $2.00 to your order for shipping.
Prices are subject to change without notice.